Keto After Age 50

Affordable, Easy & Delicious Keto Recipes | Lose Weight, Reverse Disease & Feel Younger | 30-Day Meal Plan to Kickstart Your Healthy Lifestyle

Dr Sander Hort

© Copyright 2020 Dr Sander Hort - All Rights Reserved.

In no way is it legal to reproduce, duplicate, or transmit any part of this document by either electronic means or in printed format. Recording of this publication is strictly prohibited, and any storage of this material is not allowed unless with written permission from the publisher. All rights reserved.

The information provided herein is stated to be truthful and consistent, in that any liability, regarding inattention or otherwise, by any usage or abuse of any policies, processes, or directions contained within is the solitary and complete responsibility of the recipient reader. Under no circumstances will any legal liability or blame be held against the publisher for any reparation, damages, or monetary loss due to the information herein, either directly or indirectly.

Respective authors own all copyrights not held by the publisher.

Legal Notice:

This book is copyright protected. This is only for personal use. You cannot amend, distribute, sell, use, quote or paraphrase any part of the content within this book without the consent of the author or copyright owner. Legal action will be pursued if this is breached.

Disclaimer Notice:

Please note the information contained within this document is for educational and entertainment purposes only. Every attempt has been made to provide accurate, up-to-date and reliable, complete information. No warranties of any kind are expressed or implied. Readers acknowledge that the author is not engaging in the rendering of legal, financial, medical or professional advice.

By reading this document, the reader agrees that under no circumstances are we responsible for any losses, direct or indirect, which are incurred as a result of the use of information contained within this document, including, but not limited to, errors, omissions, or inaccuracies.

Table of contents

Introduction 7
Chapter 1: The Basics of a Keto Diet 8
    What is the keto diet? 8
    How keto is different from other diets 8
    How does the ketogenic diet work? 8
    How to know you are in ketosis 9
    Benefits of a keto diet for those over 50 10
    How does aging affect your nutritional needs? 12
    How to start a keto diet when you are over 50 13
Chapter 2: What Can You Eat When You Are over 50? 15
Chapter 3: What You Can't Eat When You Are over 50? 17
Chapter 4: 30-Day Keto Meal Plan for People over 50 18
Chapter 5: Breakfast 21
    Tasty Omelet Chaffle 21
    Breakfast Omelet 22
    Mexican Frittata 23
    Protein Waffle 25
    Breakfast Muffins 26
    Chocó Peanut Butter Waffle 27
    Cheese Jalapeno Muffins 28
    Sausage Cheese Chaffle 29
    Tomato Frittata 30
    Chocó Chips Waffle 31
    Cheese Jalapeno Bread 32
    Easy Halloumi Cheese Chaffle 34
    Pumpkin Cinnamon Muffins 35
    Cheese Cauliflower Hash Browns 36
    Almond Flour Waffle 37
Chapter 6: Appetizers & Snacks 38
    Cheese Stuffed Mushrooms 38
    Delicious Chicken Alfredo Dip 39

Guacamole 40

Perfect Cucumber Salsa 41

Creamy Avocado Sauce 42

Zucchini Tots 43

Avocado Yogurt Dip 44

Keto Macadamia Hummus 45

Easy & Perfect Meatballs 46

Eggplant Chips 47

Creamy Crab Dip 48

Healthy Chicken Fritters 49

Chapter 7: Beef, Pork & Lamb 50

Easy Steak Bites 50

Hearty Beef Casserole 51

Delicious Taco Casserole 52

Flavorful Pulled Pork 53

Tasty Pork Bites 54

Shredded Cilantro Lime Pork 56

Grilled Lamb Chops 57

Pork Tacos 58

Italian Lamb Chops 59

Pork Stir Fry 60

Meatballs 61

Easy Pork Tenderloin 62

Chapter 8: Poultry 63

Chicken Avocado Salad 63

Paprika Chicken 64

Parmesan Chicken 65

Delicious Chicken Wings 66

Lemon Chicken 67

Yummy Chicken Skewers 68

Tasty Shredded Chicken 69

Flavorful Herb Chicken 70

- Tasty Shredded Chicken ... 71
- Chicken Bacon Salad ... 72

Chapter 9: Seafood ... 73
- Grilled Mahi Mahi ... 73
- Crab Salad ... 75
- Garlic Shrimp ... 77
- Easy Seafood Salad ... 79
- Easy Crab Cakes ... 80
- Nutritious Tuna Patties ... 81
- Quick Butter Cod ... 82
- Baked Tilapia ... 83
- Shrimp Avocado Salad ... 84
- Paprika Shrimp ... 85

Chapter 10: Soups & Sides ... 86
- Creamy Asparagus Soup ... 86
- Healthy Celery Soup ... 88
- Flavorful Cauliflower Soup ... 89
- Basil Zucchini Soup ... 91
- Warm & Delicious Chicken Soup ... 92
- Creamy Mushroom Soup ... 94
- Flavorful Kale Cauliflower Soup ... 95
- Delicious Pumpkin Soup ... 97
- Chicken Cauliflower Soup ... 98
- Creamy Cauliflower Mashed ... 99

Chapter 11: Desserts ... 100
- Mug Cake ... 100
- Chocó Fat Bombs ... 101
- Delicious Chocolate Frosty ... 102
- Strawberry Mousse ... 103
- Cheesecake Mousse ... 104
- Delicious Berry Cheese Dessert ... 105
- Chocó Peanut Butter Fudge ... 106

Raspberry Fat Bombs 107
Quick Lemon Mug Cake 108
Smooth & Silky Tiramisu Mousse 109
Conclusion 110

Introduction

Today's worlds are becoming a more health-conscious and finding way to maintain their healthy weight. Due to the increase in pollution, most of the peoples face a health-related issue like stress, obesity, and hypertension. These health issues are occurring due to unhealthy eating habits.

Keto diet is popular in the 1920s and 1930s used for the therapy of epilepsy. It also used in the treatment of cancer patients; keto prevents cancer cells from using glucose from energy. It starves cancer cells and prevents the growth of cells. Recent research and study prove that the keto diet has used to cure various conditions like Alzheimer's, Parkinson's, epilepsy, metabolic syndrome, obesity, high blood pressure. Keto diet also helps to maintain the blood sugar level in type-2 diabetes patients.

Keto diet is not just a diet it is one of the healthy eating habits and lifestyles. Keto diet is very effective in rapid weight loss. Normally our body uses glucose as a primary source of energy. When you are on the keto diet you consume low carb food. It will reduce the glucose level into your body. Your body burns stored fats for fuel instead of glucose.

This book guides you on how to adopt a keto diet after the age of 50 and what are the health benefits of the diet. My goal here is that provides you all related information about keto diet after age 50. After reading this book you should understand what to eat and what to avoid during the ketogenic diet.

Chapter 1: The Basics of a Keto Diet

What is the keto diet?

The keto is the short form of ketogenic, keto is basically a low carbohydrate diet which is high in fats and uses an adequate amount of proteins. Our body needs energy to perform daily activities and these energies are consuming from food in the form of carbohydrates, fats, and proteins. Basically, our body uses glucose (carbohydrates) as a primary source of energy. Glucose is

Keto diet is a low-carb high-fat diet. It consumes most of the energy from fats and proteins. Keto diet forces our body to burn fats for energy instead of glucose. This helps to push our body into the metabolic state called ketosis. It is one of the natural processes when food intake is low. Where our body produces ketones by breakdown fats in the liver and these ketones are used as a primary energy source.

How keto is different from other diets

The keto diet works effectively during the weight loss process. It is one of the low-carb diets, normally our body uses glucose for energy. Due to low-carb intake our body breakdown fats for energy. This will help to reduce the weight of the body.

Keto provides huge benefits compared to other diet plans. It not only helps to maintain your weight but also very effective in treating various illness conditions like epilepsy, metabolic syndrome, Parkinson's disease, high blood pressure. It also helps to maintain body glucose levels in type-2 diabetes.

Keto diet provides long term health benefits compare to other diet plans. During keto diet near about 75 to 90 percent of calories comes from fats, an adequate number of calories 5 to 20 percent comes from proteins and 5 percent of calories from carb intake.

How does the ketogenic diet work?

The main aim of the ketogenic diet is to push and keep your body into the metabolic state called ketosis. Normally our body consumes energy from glucose(carbohydrates) and the excess glucose is stored in the form of glycogens in our body. When glycogen level increases then these glycogens are converted into fats and store into the liver.

Keto diet is a low-carb diet due to the reduction of carb our body doesn't get enough glucose for feeding muscles and brain. The reduction of carb intake also decreases hormonal insulin levels into our bodies. During this process, our body releases fatty acids from stored fats. The liver converts these fats into molecules called ketones. These ketones supply to the muscles and brain for energy.

How to know you are in ketosis

During a ketogenic diet, our body shows various signs and symptoms which confirms that your body is in the metabolic state known as ketosis. Some signs and symptoms are as below.

- Rapid weight loss

when our body enters the ketosis state. Due to the low-carb diet glycogens store are decrease rapidly from your body. These glycogens are mostly of water; one molecule of glucose holds three molecules of water. Due to this, you lose your water weight rapidly. Losing weight during the ketogenic diet is a good sign that ensures that you are into ketosis.

- Bad breath

This is one of the common signs occurs during the process of fat breaking. In this process acetones are released from the mouth due to this you have to face bad breath problems during the diet. Acetone is used by nail polish maker it smells like gasoline, fruity and sweet. This problem basically occurs during the first week of the ketogenic diet. It goes away after some weeks during the keto diet. This problem is not happening with everyone it is one of the common side effects of ketosis. This is one of another good signs indicates that your body is in the state of ketosis.

- Dry mouth and increased thirst

During the diet, most people feel thirstier than usual. This may occur because of carb restrictions and the production of ketones. Due to this your body rapidly loses water and the body leads to dehydration. One of the reasons is that when you are in ketosis your body insulin level decreases. Due to this, your kidney releases sodium and water from your body. This is one of the signs indicates that your body is in the state of ketosis.

- Increased focus and energy

Long term ketogenic dieters notice that increase in focus and energy. When you are in the ketosis your body burns fats for energy instead of glucose. Instead of glucose, your brain burns ketones for energy. This is happening due to stable blood sugar levels and more stable energy levels because of increased ketone levels. This is also a good sign indicates you are in the state of ketosis.

- Increase urination

Increase frequent urination due to a decrease in body insulin level and your body release more sodium and water. When you are in ketosis your body losses glycogens from the body these glycogens hold 3 to 4 parts of water in it. Due to this urination is increased during ketosis. This is one of the good signs ensures that your body is in the state of ketosis.

- Insomnia

This problem is occurring when you are adopting the keto diet the first time. You are experiencing difficulty to fall asleep at night. Ketogenic diet interrupts a person's sleeping habits. This insomnia symptom typically is gone within some weeks of the ketogenic diet.

Benefits of a keto diet for those over 50

Keto diet has various health benefits for those people who are over 50 these health benefits are described as follows:

- Effective weight loss

Most of the people faces overweight problem due to extra body fats. Glucose(carbohydrates) is the primary energy source of our body. Excess glucose is converted into the form of glycogens and excess glycogens are converted and stored in the form of fats. Keto diet is carb restrictive diets due to this glucose level are decreased. In this condition, our body breaks down fats for energy. This will help to reduce body weight. Due to this reason keto is an effective weight loss diet for over 50 peoples.

- Maintain blood sugar level

Most of the over 50 peoples face an unbalanced blood sugar level. Keto diet is very effective in type-2 diabetic patients. It uses ketones for the primary source of energy instead of glucose. Glucose needs insulin to transport into body cells. Ketones don't need insulin to transport into body cells. This will make keto diet insulin resistant. Due to this keto diet helps to maintain your blood sugar level throughout the day.

- Improve your brain functions

Most of the research study proves that a keto diet improves your brain health and brain functions. It helps to reduce the risk of Parkinson's, epilepsy, neurodegeneration, and Alzheimer's conditions. Keto diet helps to decrease the level of glucose and insulin from your body. The liver produces ketones from fatty acids. Ketones provide about 70 percent of brain energy needs.

One of the research studies randomly conducted on 23 older adults with low carb and high carb diet for 6 weeks. The results show the improvement of low carb dieters.

- Treat / Prevent various diseases

Keto diet uses ketones as a primary source of energy instead of glucose. Ketones have antioxidant and anti-inflammatory properties. Due to this, it helps to treat/prevent various conditions like Alzheimer's, Parkinson's, cancer, heart-related disease, and type-2 diabetes. It also improves your heart health by increasing HDL (good cholesterol) and reducing LDL (bad cholesterol) levels.

- Reduce the risk of cancer

One of the research studies proves that your body's blood sugar under control due to the ketogenic diet or diabetic drugs may help to improve conditions from certain cancers by improving the efficiency of chemotherapy. Keto causes more oxidative stress in cancer cells to compare to normal cells.

- Increase HDL level

HDL is known as High-Density Lipoprotein. It is also known as good cholesterol. Keto diet helps to increase the level of HDL this will help to reduce the risk of heart-related disease. The ketogenic diet is one of the low-carb high-fat diets. The best way to increase HDL cholesterol levels in your body is by increasing the intake of fat. Low-carb diet plans help to increase HDL levels.

- Increase lifespan

During the ketogenic diet, insulin levels decrease this will allows your body to use ketones for energy. Lowering oxidative stress and insulin level helps to increase your lifespan. One of the research studies proves that at the time of starvation our body produces a chemical compound known as hydroxybutyrate plays an important role in the process of aging. Daily calorie restrictions are slow down the aging process and increase your lifespan.

How does aging affect your nutritional needs?

Nutrition plays a very important role to maintain our health. If you consume unhealthy food you are suffering from nutritional deficiency this will leads you to poor quality of lifestyle.
At the age of childhood, our body needs essential nutrients along with regular nutrients. Childhood is the stage in which you have to learn and experiencing food taste which makes their eating habits in the future.
At the age of teenage, most of the children attract with junk food. Encourage them to have healthy snacks to fight carving and hunger. At the age of adulthood, you must focus to maintain your body. In this stage, your body absorbs good nutrients like calcium, proteins, and vitamins. In this stage, you have to focus on your nutritional needs. This will help you to maintain your ideal body weight.
Aging affects your nutritional needs because of the variety of changes occurs into your body

like loss of muscles, lack of stomach acid and thinner skin. Aging also affects your metabolic rate it goes down.

During aging, your body needs more nutrients, proteins, vitamins, and minerals. You should follow a balanced and varied diet to fill full your nutritional needs. After 50, your body's ability to absorb vitamins is fade. For example; your body unable to break down b12 vitamins from your food source. This is happening because of the lack of stomach acid. Another example is about vitamin D, due to aging your skin less able than younger skin to absorb sunlight and convert it into vitamin D. This will affect the ability of absorption of calcium.

To stay hydrated drink plenty of water daily regardless of thirst sensation because older age people may not feel thirsty. Nutrition changes occur throughout our lives. Just follow some key principles that will keep you healthy. Enjoy a variety of nutritious and healthy foods with the company of family and friends.

How to start a keto diet when you are over 50

If you are over 50 and think about weight loss, then keto is the best choice for you. You can achieve this by following one kind of diet known as the keto diet. Keto diet helps to burn body fat effectively. You can lose weight effectively without doing any hard work out in the gym.

The ketogenic diet is working for every type of health issue and background like obesity, blood sugar issues. At the age of over 50, your metabolism works too slow to burn extra fats and calories. This is one of the realities but it doesn't mean that the person over age 50 cannot follow the ketogenic lifestyle. The ketogenic diet is a varied diet plan; you just follow some changes in it. Following some simple rules, you can adopt a ketogenic diet without finding any difficulty.

- Consume low-carb foods are the main aim of the ketogenic diet. It allows 5 to 10 percent of carb (20 gm) in your meal.
- Increase the consumption of fatty meals. You have to consume high-fat breakfast consisting of avocado, eggs, bacon, and coffee mixed with high-fat butter.
- Don't consume high protein during the ketogenic diet. It recommends only an adequate amount of protein. You can consume fatty meats like lamb, salmon, pork,

beef, eggs, chicken, etc.
- Don't count calories for the first three weeks. Eat healthy food until you are satisfied and not feeling hungry anymore. After three weeks check your body weight. If the bodyweight decrease, then keeps following this rule.
- Always keep track of your weight during a keto diet. If weight decreases, then it is a sign that you are on the right path. Another method to track you are in ketosis or not is a blood ketone test. This test clearly indicates that you are in ketosis or not.

Chapter 2: What Can You Eat When You Are over 50?

As we know that the ketogenic diet is low carb high fat and an adequate amount of protein diet. The following is the food list that allows during the keto diet.

Fats: Fat is necessary during keto diet because near about 75 to 90percent of calories come from fat.

- Oils: Instead of processed oil, use oils come from seeds and nuts some keto-friendly oils are coconut oil, butter, avocado oil, MCT oils, lard, extra virgin olive oil, and macadamia oils.
- Nuts and seeds: Nuts and seeds are one of the best choices during keto diet because it is high in fat and low in carb. Some keto-friendly nuts and seeds are brazil nuts, pecans, hazelnuts, walnuts, macadamia nuts, pumpkin seeds, flaxseeds, chia seeds, sesame seeds, almonds, and hemp seeds.

Proteins: Adequate amount of proteins (5 to 20 %) are needed during the ketogenic diet.

- Meat: Organic and grass-fed meats prefer during the keto diet. Unprocessed meats are low in carb and high in protein. Beef, pork, wild game, veal, and lamb are the best choices for the keto diet.
- Poultry: Chicken, Cornish hen, pheasant, quails, duck, turkey, and eggs are the best choices during the keto diet.
- Seafood: Salmon, cod, catfish, mahi-mahi, halibut, tuna, trout, octopus, oyster, clams, and shellfish are the best choice during the keto diet.
- Dairy: Use high-fat dairy products instead of low fat because the low-fat dairy product contains added sugar. Heavy cream, butter, yogurt, parmesan cheese, cheddar cheese, feta cheese, Colby cheese, mascarpone, Swiss cheese, and mozzarella is the healthy choice during the keto diet.

Carbohydrates: Keto diet is a low carb diet it requires 5 percent of calories from carb intake.

- Fruits: Low calories fruits are preferred during the keto diet. Avocado, lemon, blackberries, raspberries, watermelon, and strawberry are the best choices during the keto diet.
- Vegetables: Green and leafy vegetables are one of the healthiest choices during keto diet because they are low in carb and high in nutrients. Spinach, chives, asparagus, radicchio, broccoli, cabbage, Brussels sprout, zucchini, celery, chard, bell peppers, olives, etc.
- Drinks: During keto diet drink plenty of water to keep your body hydrated. You can also drink plain water, coconut milk, lemon water, almond milk, and low-carb juices.
- Condiments: Condiments are used for flavor, you can use low-carb marinara sauce, soy sauce, unsweetened ketchup, yellow mustard all these condiments are no added sugar.

Chapter 3: What You Can't Eat When You Are over 50?

Here is a list of foods that should avoid during ketogenic diet

- Fats to avoid

Avoid refined oils they contain omega-6 fatty acids which raise your blood pressure. Soybean oil, sunflower oil, peanut oil, corn oil, sesame oil, margarine, grape-seed oil. Also, avoid packed foods that contain processed Trans fats.

- Protein to avoid

Avoid processed meats, packed sausage, canned meat, smoked meat, beef jerky, hotdogs, fatless cheese, sweetened yogurt, salami.

- Carb to avoid

Avoid starchy vegetables like potato, parsnip, beets, yucca, corn, peas and sweet potato these vegetables are high in carb.
Avoid Fruits like mango, pear, dates, raisins, grapes, pineapple, apple are high in carb and sugar.
Avoid legumes and beans like black beans, kidney beans, fava beans, lima beans, chickpeas, pinto beans, oatmeal, lentils, and cereals. It contains high-carb values.
Avoid whole grains like wheat, rice, bulgur, quinoa, oat, barley, and buckwheat.

- Sweeteners to avoid

Avoid maple syrup, agave nectar, honey, sugar, corn syrup, sucralose, and Splenda.

- Drinks to avoid

During keto diet avoid sweetened and processed drinks like tea, coffee, soda, sugar, milk and fruit juices. Avoid Alcohol like liquor, beer, sweetened cocktail, and wine. It is also responsible to rise in blood sugar.

Chapter 4: 30-Day Keto Meal Plan for People over 50

Day 1

Breakfast-Tasty Omelet Chaffle

Lunch-Baked Tilapia

Dinner-Parmesan Chicken

Day 2

Breakfast-Breakfast Omelet

Lunch-Basil Zucchini Soup

Dinner-Pork Stir Fry

Day 3

Breakfast-Mexican Frittata

Lunch-Chicken Avocado Salad

Dinner-Pork Tacos

Day 4

Breakfast-Protein Waffle

Lunch-Chicken Bacon Salad

Dinner-Quick Butter Cod

Day 5

Breakfast-Breakfast Muffins

Lunch-Chicken Cauliflower Soup

Dinner-Shredded Cilantro Lime Pork

Day 6

Breakfast-Chocó Peanut Butter Waffle

Lunch-Crab Salad

Dinner-Shrimp Avocado Salad

Day 7

Breakfast-Cheese Jalapeno Muffins

Lunch-Creamy Asparagus Soup

Dinner-Tasty Pork Bites

Day 8

Breakfast-Sausage Cheese Chaffle

Lunch-Creamy Cauliflower Mashed

Dinner-Tasty Shredded Chicken

Day 9

Breakfast-Tomato Frittata

Lunch-Creamy Mushroom Soup

Dinner-Warm & Delicious Chicken Soup

Day 10

Breakfast-Chocó Chips Waffle

Lunch-Delicious Chicken Wings

Dinner-Yummy Chicken Skewers

Day 11

Breakfast-Cheese Jalapeno Bread

Lunch-Delicious Pumpkin Soup

Dinner-Paprika Chicken

Day 12

Breakfast-Easy Halloumi Cheese Chaffle

Lunch-Delicious Taco Casserole

Dinner-Nutritious Tuna Patties

Day 13

Breakfast-Pumpkin Cinnamon Muffins

Lunch-Easy Crab Cakes

Dinner-Meatballs

Day 14

Breakfast-Cheese Cauliflower Hash Browns

Lunch-Easy Pork Tenderloin

Dinner-Lemon Chicken

Day 15

Breakfast-Almond Flour Waffle

Lunch-Easy Seafood Salad

Dinner-Italian Lamb Chops

Day 16

Breakfast-Almond Flour Waffle

Lunch-Easy Steak Bites

Dinner-Hearty Beef Casserole

Day 17

Breakfast-Cheese Cauliflower Hash Browns

Lunch-Flavorful Cauliflower Soup

Dinner-Healthy Celery Soup

Day 18

Breakfast-Pumpkin Cinnamon Muffins

Lunch-Flavorful Herb Chicken

Dinner-Grilled Mahi Mahi

Day 19

Breakfast-Easy Halloumi Cheese Chaffle

Lunch-Flavorful Kale Cauliflower Soup

Dinner-Grilled Lamb Chops

Day 20

Breakfast-Cheese Jalapeno Bread

Lunch-Flavorful Pulled Pork

Dinner-Garlic Shrimp

Day 21

Breakfast-Chocó Chips Waffle

Lunch-Garlic Shrimp

Dinner-Flavorful Pulled Pork

Day 22

Breakfast-Tomato Frittata

Lunch-Grilled Lamb Chops

Dinner-Flavorful Kale Cauliflower Soup

Day 23

Breakfast-Sausage Cheese Chaffle

Lunch-Grilled Mahi Mahi

Dinner-Flavorful Herb Chicken

Day 24

Breakfast-Cheese Jalapeno Muffins

Lunch-Healthy Celery Soup

Dinner-Flavorful Cauliflower Soup

Day 25

Breakfast-Chocó Peanut Butter Waffle

Lunch-Hearty Beef Casserole

Dinner-Easy Steak Bites

Day 26

Breakfast-Breakfast Muffins

Lunch-Italian Lamb Chops

Dinner-Easy Seafood Salad

Day 27

Breakfast-Protein Waffle

Lunch-Lemon Chicken

Dinner-Easy Pork Tenderloin

Day 28

Breakfast-Mexican Frittata

Lunch-Meatballs

Dinner-Easy Crab Cakes

Day 29

Breakfast-Breakfast Omelet

Lunch-Nutritious Tuna Patties

Dinner-Delicious Taco Casserole

Day 30

Breakfast-Tasty Omelet Chaffle

Lunch-Paprika Chicken

Dinner-Delicious Pumpkin Soup

Chapter 5: Breakfast

Tasty Omelet Chaffle

Preparation Time: 5 minutes
Cooking Time: 3 minutes
Serve: 1

Ingredients:

- 2 eggs, lightly beaten
- 1 tbsp bell pepper, chopped
- 1 tbsp ham, chopped
- 2 tbsp cheddar cheese, shredded
- 2 tbsp almond milk
- Pepper
- Salt

Directions:

1. Preheat the waffle maker.
2. In a bowl, whisk eggs. Add remaining ingredients and stir well.
3. Spray waffle maker with cooking spray.
4. Pour batter in the hot waffle maker and cook for 2-3 minutes or until set.
5. Serve and enjoy.

Nutritional Value (Amount per Serving):

- Calories 304
- Fat 21.6 g
- Carbohydrates 11.9 g
- Sugar 7.8 g
- Protein 17.9 g
- Cholesterol 347 mg

Breakfast Omelet

Preparation Time: 10 minutes
Cooking Time: 5 minutes
Serve: 4

Ingredients:

- 4 large eggs
- 2 oz cheddar cheese, shredded
- 8 olives, pitted
- 2 tbsp butter
- 2 tbsp olive oil
- 1 tsp herb de Provence
- 1/2 tsp salt

Directions:

1. Whisk eggs in a bowl with salt, olives, herb de Provence, and olive oil.
2. Melt butter in a large pan over medium heat.
3. Pour egg mixture into the hot pan and spread evenly.
4. Cover and cook for 3 minutes or until omelet lightly golden brown.
5. Flip omelet to the other side and cook for 2 minutes more.
6. Serve and enjoy.

Nutritional Value (Amount per Serving):

- Calories 251
- Fat 22 g
- Carbohydrates 1.1 g
- Sugar 0.6 g
- Protein 10.2 g
- Cholesterol 215 mg

Mexican Frittata

Preparation Time: 10 minutes
Cooking Time: 20 minutes
Serve: 6

Ingredients:

- 8 eggs, scrambled
- 1/2 cup salsa
- 2 tsp taco seasoning, homemade
- 1/2 lb ground beef
- 1/2 cup cheddar cheese, grated
- 2 tbsp green onion, chopped
- 1/3 lb tomatoes, sliced
- 1 small green pepper, chopped
- 1 tbsp olive oil
- 1/4 tsp salt

Directions:

1. Preheat the oven to 375 F.
2. Heat oil in a pan over medium heat.
3. Add beef and sauté until browned.
4. Add salsa and taco seasoning and stir to coat.
5. Remove meat from the pan and place on a plate.
6. Add green pepper to the pan and cook for a few minutes.
7. Return meat to the pan along with green onion and tomato.
8. Add scrambled eggs on top then sprinkle with grated cheese.
9. Bake for 20-25 minutes.
10. Serve and enjoy.

Nutritional Value (Amount per Serving):

- Calories 227

- Fat 13.8 g
- Carbohydrates 4 g
- Sugar 2.3 g
- Protein 22 g
- Cholesterol 262 mg

Protein Waffle

Preparation Time: 5 minutes
Cooking Time: 10 minutes
Serve: 2

Ingredients:

- 1 egg, lightly beaten
- 1 tbsp almond milk
- 1 scoop protein powder
- 1/4 tsp baking powder, gluten-free
- 1 tbsp butter, melted
- 1/4 tsp salt

Directions:

1. Add all ingredients in a bowl and mix until combined.
2. Spray waffle maker with cooking spray.
3. Pour half of the batter in the hot waffle maker and cook until golden brown. Repeat with the remaining batter.
4. Serve and enjoy.

Nutritional Value (Amount per Serving):

- Calories 160
- Fat 10.7 g
- Carbohydrates 2.7 g
- Sugar 0.9 g
- Protein 14.1 g
- Cholesterol 129 mg

Breakfast Muffins

Preparation Time: 15 minutes
Cooking Time: 25 minutes
Serve: 6

Ingredients:

- 12 eggs
- 1/2 cup fresh spinach, shredded
- 1/4 tsp garlic powder
- 3/4 cup ham, diced and cooked
- 3 tbsp onion, chopped
- 1 cup cheddar cheese, shredded
- 1/4 cup mushrooms, chopped and sautéed
- 1/4 cup bell pepper, diced
- 1/4 tsp pepper
- 1/2 tsp salt

Directions:

1. Preheat the oven to 350 F.
2. Spray a muffin tray with cooking spray and set aside.
3. In a large bowl, beat eggs. Add remaining ingredients to the bowl and mix well together.
4. Pour egg mixture into the prepared muffin tray.
5. Bake for 20-25 minutes.
6. Serve and enjoy.

Nutritional Value (Amount per Serving):

- Calories 243
- Fat 17 g
- Carbohydrates 2.8 g
- Sugar 1.3 g
- Protein 19.8 g
- Cholesterol 360 mg

Chocó Peanut Butter Waffle

Preparation Time: 5 minutes
Cooking Time: 10 minutes
Serve: 4

Ingredients:

- 4 eggs, lightly beaten
- 2 1/2 tbsp unsweetened cocoa powder
- 1/4 cup lakanto monk fruit
- 1/2 cup almond flour
- 1/3 cup unsweetened peanut butter
- 1/2 tsp baking powder, gluten-free

Directions:

1. Preheat the waffle maker.
2. Add all ingredients in a medium bowl and mix until well combined.
3. Spray waffle maker with cooking spray.
4. Pour 1/4 cup of batter in the hot waffle maker and cook until golden brown. Repeat with the remaining batter.
5. Serve and enjoy.

Nutritional Value (Amount per Serving):

- Calories 271
- Fat 20 g
- Carbohydrates 6.5 g
- Sugar 1 g
- Protein 13.5 g
- Cholesterol 186 mg

Cheese Jalapeno Muffins

Preparation Time: 10 minutes
Cooking Time: 20 minutes
Serve: 12

Ingredients:

- 9 eggs
- 6 bacon slices, cooked and chopped
- 3/4 cup heavy cream
- 1 1/2 jalapeno pepper, sliced
- 8.5 oz cheddar cheese, shredded
- Pepper
- Salt

Directions:

1. Preheat the oven to 350 F.
2. Spray a muffin tray with cooking spray and add cooked bacon slices to each muffin cup.
3. In a large bowl, whisk together eggs, cheese, cream, pepper, and salt.
4. Pour egg mixture into the prepared muffin tray.
5. Add sliced jalapeno into each muffin cup.
6. Bake for 15-20 minutes.
7. Serve and enjoy.

Nutritional Value (Amount per Serving):

- Calories 228
- Fat 18.4 g
- Carbohydrates 1 g
- Sugar 0.4 g
- Protein 14.3 g
- Cholesterol 169 mg

Sausage Cheese Chaffle

Preparation Time: 5 minutes
Cooking Time: 15 minutes
Serve: 6

Ingredients:

- 1/2 lb Italian sausage
- 1/2 cup cheddar cheese, shredded
- 1/2 cup almond flour
- 1 egg, lightly beaten
- 2 tbsp parmesan cheese, grated

Directions:

1. Preheat waffle maker.
2. Add all ingredients into the bowl and mix until well combined.
3. Spray waffle maker with cooking spray.
4. Pour 3 tbsp of batter in the hot waffle maker and cook until golden brown. Repeat with the remaining batter.
5. Serve and enjoy.

Nutritional Value (Amount per Serving):

- Calories 234
- Fat 19.4 g
- Carbohydrates 2.6 g
- Sugar 0.4 g
- Protein 12.9 g
- Cholesterol 70 mg

Tomato Frittata

Preparation Time: 10 minutes
Cooking Time: 13 minutes
Serve: 2

Ingredients:

- 6 eggs
- 2/3 cup cherry tomatoes, halved
- 2/3 cup feta cheese, crumbled
- 1 small onion, sliced
- 1 tbsp chives, chopped
- 1 ½ tbsp basil, chopped
- 1 tbsp butter
- Pepper
- Salt

Directions:

1. Preheat the oven to 400 F.
2. Melt butter in a pan over medium heat.
3. Add onion to the pan and sauté until lightly browned.
4. In a bowl, whisk eggs with chives, basil, pepper, and salt.
5. Once onions are done then add egg mixture and cook for 2-3 minutes.
6. Top with cheese and cherry tomatoes. Place in oven and cook for 5-7 minutes.
7. Serve and enjoy.

Nutritional Value (Amount per Serving):

- Calories 394
- Fat 29.7 g
- Carbohydrates 8.1 g
- Sugar 5.9 g
- Protein 24.7 g
- Cholesterol 551 mg

Chocó Chips Waffle

Preparation Time: 5 minutes
Cooking Time: 15 minutes
Serve: 2

Ingredients:

- 3 eggs
- 1/4 cup Swerve
- 1/2 cup butter
- 1/2 cup unsweetened chocolate chips
- 1/2 tsp vanilla

Directions:

1. Preheat the waffle maker.
2. Add chocolate chips and butter in microwave-safe bowl and microwave for 1 minute. Stir well.
3. In a bowl, whisk eggs with vanilla and Swerve until frothy.
4. Add melted butter and chocolate mixture in the egg mixture and stir well.
5. Spray waffle maker with cooking spray.
6. Pour 1/4 batter in the hot waffle maker and cook for 6-8 minutes or until golden brown. Repeat with the remaining batter.
7. Serve and enjoy.

Nutritional Value (Amount per Serving):

- Calories 670
- Fat 69.9 g
- Carbohydrates 10.8 g
- Sugar 1 g
- Protein 13 g
- Cholesterol 368 mg

Cheese Jalapeno Bread

Preparation Time: 10 minutes
Cooking Time: 15 minutes
Serve: 4

Ingredients:

- 4 eggs
- 1/3 cup coconut flour
- 1/4 cup water
- 1/4 cup butter
- 1/4 tsp pepper
- 3 jalapeno chilies, chopped
- ¼ tsp onion powder
- 1/2 cup cheddar cheese, grated
- 1/4 cup parmesan cheese, grated
- 1/4 tsp baking powder, gluten-free
- 1/2 tsp garlic powder
- 1/2 tsp salt

Directions:

1. Preheat the oven to 400 F.
2. In a bowl, mix together eggs, pepper, salt, water, and butter.
3. Add baking powder, garlic powder, onion powder, and coconut flour and mix well.
4. Add jalapenos, cheddar cheese, and parmesan cheese. Mix well and season with pepper.
5. Line baking tray with parchment pepper.
6. Pour batter into a baking tray and spread evenly.
7. Bake for 15 minutes.
8. Slice and serve.

Nutritional Value (Amount per Serving):

- Calories 249
- Fat 22 g
- Carbohydrates 2.7 g
- Sugar 1.1 g
- Protein 11.1 g
- Cholesterol 233 mg

Easy Halloumi Cheese Chaffle

Preparation Time: 5 minutes
Cooking Time: 10 minutes
Serve: 2

Ingredients:

- 3 oz Halloumi cheese, cut into 1/2-inch thick slices

Directions:

1. Place cheese slice in the waffle maker and cook for 5-6 minutes or until golden brown. Repeat with the remaining cheese slice.
2. Serve and enjoy.

Nutritional Value (Amount per Serving):

- Calories 155
- Fat 12.7 g
- Carbohydrates 1.1 g
- Sugar 1.1 g
- Protein 9.2 g
- Cholesterol 34 mg

Pumpkin Cinnamon Muffins

Preparation Time: 10 minutes

Cooking Time: 15 minutes

Serve: 20

Ingredients:

- 1/2 cup pumpkin puree
- 1/2 cup almond butter
- 1 tbsp cinnamon
- 1/2 cup coconut oil
- 1 tsp baking powder
- 2 scoops vanilla protein powder
- 1/2 cup almond flour

Directions:

1. Preheat the oven to 350 F.
2. Spray a muffin tray with cooking spray and set aside.
3. In a large bowl, mix together all dry ingredients.
4. Add wet ingredients into the dry ingredients and mix until well combined.
5. Pour batter into the prepared muffin tray and bake for 15 minutes.
6. Serve and enjoy.

Nutritional Value (Amount per Serving):

- Calories 81
- Fat 7.1 g
- Carbohydrates 1.5 g
- Sugar 0.5 g
- Protein 3.5 g
- Cholesterol 0 mg

Cheese Cauliflower Hash Browns

Preparation Time: 10 minutes
Cooking Time: 15 minutes
Serve: 6

Ingredients:

- 3 cups cauliflower, grated
- 3/4 cup cheddar cheese, shredded
- 1 egg, lightly beaten
- 1/2 tsp garlic powder
- 1/2 tsp cayenne pepper
- 1/4 tsp pepper
- 1/2 tsp salt

Directions:

1. Add all ingredients into the bowl and mix until well combined.
2. Spray a baking tray with cooking spray and set aside.
3. Make six hash browns from cauliflower mixture and place on a prepared baking tray.
4. Bake at 400 F for 15 minutes.
5. Serve and enjoy.

Nutritional Value (Amount per Serving):

- Calories 81
- Fat 5 g
- Carbohydrates 3.1 g
- Sugar 1 g
- Protein 5.3 g
- Cholesterol 46 mg

Almond Flour Waffle

Preparation Time: 5 minutes
Cooking Time: 10 minutes
Serve: 4

Ingredients:

- 1 cup almond flour
- 4 eggs, lightly beaten
- 1/4 cup heavy cream
- Pinch of salt

Directions:

1. Preheat the waffle maker.
2. Add all ingredients in a bowl and whisk until well combined.
3. Spray waffle maker with cooking spray.
4. Pour 1/4 batter in the hot waffle maker and cook until golden brown. Repeat with the remaining batter.
5. Serve and enjoy.

Nutritional Value (Amount per Serving):

- Calories 249
- Fat 21.2 g
- Carbohydrates 6.6 g
- Sugar 1.3 g
- Protein 11.7 g
- Cholesterol 174 mg

Chapter 6: Appetizers & Snacks

Cheese Stuffed Mushrooms

Preparation Time: 10 minutes
Cooking Time: 15 minutes
Serve: 12

Ingredients:

- 12 large mushrooms, clean, remove stems and chopped stems finely
- 1 ½ tbsp fresh parsley, chopped
- 4 garlic cloves, minced
- ½ cup parmesan cheese, grated
- ¼ cup Swiss cheese, grated
- 3.5 oz cream cheese
- 1 tbsp olive oil
- Salt

Directions:

1. Preheat the oven to 375 F.
2. Toss mushrooms with olive oil and place onto a baking tray.
3. In a bowl, combine cream cheese, chopped mushrooms stems, parsley, garlic, parmesan cheese, Swiss cheese, and salt.
4. Stuff cream cheese mixture into the mushroom caps and arrange mushrooms on the baking tray.
5. Bake in preheated oven for 10-15 minutes.
6. Serve and enjoy.

Nutritional Value (Amount per Serving):

- Calories 79
- Fat 6.3 g
- Carbohydrates 1.5 g
- Sugar 0.5 g
- Protein 4 g
- Cholesterol 16 mg

Delicious Chicken Alfredo Dip

Preparation Time: 10 minutes
Cooking Time: 20 minutes
Serve: 8

Ingredients:

- 2 cups chicken, cooked and chopped in small pieces
- 1 ½ tbsp fresh parsley, chopped
- 1 tomato, diced
- 2 bacon slices, cooked and crumbled
- 1 ½ cups mozzarella cheese, shredded
- 1 tsp Italian seasoning
- ½ cup parmesan cheese, grated
- 8 oz cream cheese, softened
- 1 ½ cups Alfredo sauce, homemade & low-carb

Directions:

1. Preheat the oven to 375 F.
2. Spray a baking dish with cooking spray and set aside.
3. Add chicken, ½ cup mozzarella cheese, Italian seasoning, parmesan cheese, cream cheese, and Alfredo sauce to the bowl and stir to combine.
4. Spread chicken mixture into the prepared baking dish and top with remaining mozzarella cheese.
5. Bake in preheated oven for 20 minutes.
6. Top with parsley, tomatoes, and bacon.
7. Serve and enjoy.

Nutritional Value (Amount per Serving):

- Calories 144
- Fat 0.5 g
- Carbohydrates 7.4 g
- Sugar 1.3 g
- Protein 29.3 g
- Cholesterol 216 mg

Guacamole

Preparation Time: 10 minutes
Cooking Time: 5 minutes
Serve: 8

Ingredients:

- 2 avocados, halved and pitted
- 1 tbsp fresh lemon juice
- 2 garlic cloves, minced
- ¼ tsp ground cumin
- 2 tbsp fresh parsley, chopped
- ½ jalapeno pepper, chopped
- 2 tbsp onion, chopped
- ½ tsp sea salt

Directions:

1. Scoop out avocados flesh using a spoon and place it into the bowl.
2. Mash the avocado flesh using a fork.
3. Add remaining ingredients and stir until well combined.
4. Serve and enjoy.

Nutritional Value (Amount per Serving):

- Calories 106
- Fat 9.9 g
- Carbohydrates 4.9 g
- Sugar 0.4 g
- Protein 1.1 g
- Cholesterol 0 mg

Perfect Cucumber Salsa

Preparation Time: 5 minutes
Cooking Time: 5 minutes
Serve: 10

Ingredients:

- 2 ½ cups cucumbers, peeled, seeded, and chopped
- 2 tsp fresh cilantro, chopped
- 2 tsp fresh parsley, chopped
- 1 ½ tbsp fresh lemon juice
- 1 garlic clove, minced
- 1 small onion, chopped
- 2 large jalapeno peppers, chopped
- 1 ½ cups tomatoes, chopped
- ½ tsp salt

Directions:

1. Add all ingredients into the large mixing bowl and mix until well combined.
2. Serve and enjoy.

Nutritional Value (Amount per Serving):

- Calories 14
- Fat 0.2 g
- Carbohydrates 3 g
- Sugar 1.6 g
- Protein 0.6 g
- Cholesterol 0 mg

Creamy Avocado Sauce

Preparation Time: 5 minutes
Cooking Time: 5 minutes
Serve: 8

Ingredients:

- 1 avocado, halved, seeded, and peeled
- 1 tbsp fresh lemon juice
- 2 garlic cloves
- 2 tbsp olive oil
- 3 tbsp fresh parsley, chopped
- Pepper
- Salt

Directions:

1. Add all ingredients into the food processor and process until smooth.
2. Serve and enjoy.

Nutritional Value (Amount per Serving):

- Calories 83
- Fat 8.4 g
- Carbohydrates 2.6 g
- Sugar 0.2 g
- Protein 0.6 g
- Cholesterol 0 mg

Zucchini Tots

Preparation Time: 10 minutes
Cooking Time: 20 minutes
Serve: 4

Ingredients:

- 5 cups zucchini, grated and squeeze out all liquid
- ½ tsp garlic powder
- ½ tsp dried oregano
- ½ cup parmesan cheese, grated
- ½ cup cheddar cheese, shredded
- 2 eggs, lightly beaten
- Pepper
- Salt

Directions:

1. Preheat the oven to 400 F.
2. Spray a baking tray with cooking spray and set aside.
3. Add all ingredients into the bowl and mix until well combined.
4. Make small tots from the zucchini mixture and place onto the prepared baking tray.
5. Bake in preheated oven for 15-20 minutes.
6. Serve and enjoy.

Nutritional Value (Amount per Serving):

- Calories 353
- Fat 23.1 g
- Carbohydrates 9.5 g
- Sugar 2.8 g
- Protein 32.1 g
- Cholesterol 157 mg

Avocado Yogurt Dip

Preparation Time: 5 minutes
Cooking Time: 5 minutes
Serve: 4

Ingredients:

- 2 avocados
- 1 lime juice
- 3 garlic cloves, minced
- ½ cup Greek yogurt
- Pepper
- Salt

Directions:

1. Scoop out avocado flesh using the spoon and place it in a bowl.
2. Mash avocado flesh using the fork.
3. Add remaining ingredients and stir to combine.
4. Serve and enjoy.

Nutritional Value (Amount per Serving):

- Calories 139
- Fat 11 g
- Carbohydrates 9 g
- Protein 4 g
- Sugar 2 g
- Cholesterol 15 mg

Keto Macadamia Hummus

Preparation Time: 10 minutes

Cooking Time: 5 minutes

Serve: 8

Ingredients:

- 1 cup macadamia nuts, soaked in water for overnight, drained and rinsed
- 1 ½ tbsp tahini
- 2 tbsp water
- 2 tbsp fresh lime juice
- 2 garlic cloves
- 1/8 tsp cayenne pepper
- Pepper
- Salt

Directions:

1. Add all ingredients into the food processor and process until smooth.
2. Serve and enjoy.

Nutritional Value (Amount per Serving):

- Calories 138
- Fat 14.2 g
- Carbohydrates 3.2 g
- Protein 1.9 g
- Sugar 1.9 g
- Cholesterol 0mg

Easy & Perfect Meatballs

Preparation Time: 10 minutes
Cooking Time: 20 minutes
Serve: 8

Ingredients:

- 1 egg, lightly beaten
- 3 garlic cloves, minced
- ½ cup mozzarella cheese, shredded
- ½ cup parmesan cheese, grated
- 1 lb ground beef
- Pepper
- Salt

Directions:

1. Preheat the oven to 400 F.
2. Line baking tray with parchment paper and set aside.
3. Add all ingredients into the mixing bowl and mix until well combined.
4. Make small balls from meat mixture and place on a prepared baking tray.
5. Bake in preheated oven for 20 minutes.
6. Serve and enjoy.

Nutritional Value (Amount per Serving):

- Calories 157
- Fat 6.7 g
- Carbohydrates 0.5 g
- Protein 21.5 g
- Sugar 0.1 g
- Cholesterol 80mg

Eggplant Chips

Preparation Time: 10 minutes
Cooking Time: 20 minutes
Serve: 15

Ingredients:

- 1 large eggplant, thinly sliced
- ¼ cup parmesan cheese, grated
- 1 tsp dried oregano
- ¼ tsp dried basil
- ½ tsp garlic powder
- ¼ cup olive oil
- ¼ tsp pepper
- ½ tsp salt

Directions:

1. Preheat the oven to 325 F.
2. In a small bowl, mix together oil and dried spices.
3. Coat eggplant with oil and spice mixture and arrange eggplant slices on a baking tray.
4. Bake in preheated oven for 15-20 minutes. Turn halfway through.
5. Remove from oven and sprinkle with grated cheese.
6. Serve and enjoy.

Nutritional Value (Amount per Serving):

- Calories 77
- Fat 5.8 g
- Carbohydrates 2 g
- Protein 3.5 g
- Sugar 0.9 g
- Cholesterol 8mg

Creamy Crab Dip

Preparation Time: 5 minutes
Cooking Time: 5 minutes
Serve: 16

Ingredients:

- 8 oz crab meat
- ¼ tsp garlic powder
- 2 tbsp green onion, chopped
- 1 tsp Cajun seasoning
- 1 tbsp lime juice
- ¼ cup mayonnaise
- 3.5 oz cream cheese
- ¼ tsp pepper
- ½ tsp salt

Directions:

1. Add all ingredients into the mixing bowl and whisk until well combined.
2. Serve and enjoy.

Nutritional Value (Amount per Serving):

- Calories 49
- Fat 3.6 g
- Carbohydrates 1.4 g
- Protein 2.3 g
- Sugar 0.3 g
- Cholesterol 15 mg

Healthy Chicken Fritters

Preparation Time: 10 minutes
Cooking Time: 20 minutes
Serve: 4

Ingredients:

- 1 ½ lbs chicken breast, skinless, boneless, and chopped in small pieces
- 1 tbsp olive oil
- ½ tsp garlic powder
- 2 tbsp fresh parsley, chopped
- 1 ½ tbsp chives, chopped
- 1 ½ tbsp fresh basil, chopped
- 1 cup mozzarella cheese, shredded
- 1/3 cup almond flour
- 2 eggs, lightly beaten
- Pepper
- Salt

Directions:

1. Add all ingredients except oil into the large mixing bowl and mix until well combined.
2. Heat oil in a pan over medium heat.
3. Scoop fritter mixture using a large spoon and transfer it to the pan and cook for 6-8 minutes or until golden brown on both sides.
4. Serve and enjoy.

Nutritional Value (Amount per Serving):

- Calories 331
- Fat 15.9 g
- Carbohydrates 2.9 g
- Protein 43 g
- Sugar 0.6 g
- Cholesterol 194mg

Chapter 7: Beef, Pork & Lamb

Easy Steak Bites

Preparation Time: 10 minutes
Cooking Time: 8 hours
Serve: 6

Ingredients:

- 3 lbs round steak, cut into pieces
- 1 cup chicken stock
- ¼ cup butter
- 3 garlic cloves, minced
- ½ onion, diced
- ¼ tsp pepper
- 1 tsp salt

Directions:

1. Add all ingredients into the slow cooker and stir well.
2. Cover slow cooker with lid and cook on low for 8 hours.
3. Stir well and serve.

Nutritional Value (Amount per Serving):

- Calories 565
- Fat 29.6 g
- Carbohydrates 1.6 g
- Sugar 0.5 g
- Protein 68.8 g
- Cholesterol 213 mg

Hearty Beef Casserole

Preparation Time: 10 minutes
Cooking Time: 35 minutes
Serve: 8

Ingredients:

- 1 lb ground beef
- ¾ cup mozzarella cheese, shredded
- ¾ cup cheddar cheese, shredded
- 2 cans green beans, drained
- ¼ tsp garlic powder
- ½ cup heavy whipping cream
- ½ cup chicken stock
- 3 oz cream cheese
- ¼ tsp pepper
- ½ tsp salt

Directions:

1. Preheat the oven to 350 F.
2. Brown ground meat in the pan then drains excess grease.
3. Add garlic powder, heavy whipping cream, stock, cream cheese, pepper, and salt and stir until cheese is melted. Bring to boil.
4. Turn heat to medium and cook until the meat mixture is thickened.
5. Add green beans and stir well. Sprinkle cheese on top of beans.
6. Bake for 25 minutes.
7. Serve and enjoy.

Nutritional Value (Amount per Serving):

- Calories 280
- Fat 20 g
- Carbohydrates 4 g
- Sugar 0.2 g
- Protein 18 g
- Cholesterol 88 mg

Delicious Taco Casserole

Preparation Time: 10 minutes
Cooking Time: 40 minutes
Serve: 6

Ingredients:

- 1 ½ lbs ground beef
- 8 oz cheddar cheese, shredded
- 15 oz cottage cheese
- 1 cup of salsa
- 1 ½ tbsp taco seasoning, homemade

Directions:

1. Preheat the oven to 400 F.
2. Mix taco seasoning and meat in a large casserole dish. Bake for 20 minutes.
3. Mix together cottage cheese, 1 cup cheddar cheese, and salsa and set aside.
4. Remove casserole dish from oven and break meat into pieces. Spread cottage cheese mixture on top of the meat.
5. Sprinkle remaining cheese on top.
6. Return the casserole dish to the oven and bake for 15-20 minutes.
7. Serve and enjoy.

Nutritional Value (Amount per Serving):

- Calories 438
- Fat 21 g
- Carbohydrates 5.8 g
- Sugar 1.8 g
- Protein 54.2 g
- Cholesterol 147 mg

Flavorful Pulled Pork

Preparation Time: 10 minutes
Cooking Time: 4 hours
Serve: 4

Ingredients:

- 2 lbs pork shoulder
- 1/3 cup chicken broth
- 1 ½ tsp cocoa powder
- ½ tsp ground fennel seeds
- ½ tsp cayenne
- 1 ½ tsp paprika
- 2 tsp dried rosemary
- 1 tsp garlic powder
- 2 tsp onion powder
- ¼ tsp pepper
- 1 tbsp sea salt

Directions:

1. In a small bowl, mix together cocoa powder and all spices.
2. Rub spice mixture over pork shoulder. Place pork shoulder in the slow cooker.
3. Pour broth over pork shoulder.
4. Cover slow cooker with lid and cook on high for 4 hours.
5. Remove pork from slow cooker and shred using a fork.
6. Serve and enjoy.

Nutritional Value (Amount per Serving):

- Calories 679
- Fat 49 g
- Carbohydrates 3 g
- Sugar 0.8 g
- Protein 53.8 g
- Cholesterol 204 mg

Tasty Pork Bites

Preparation Time: 10 minutes
Cooking Time: 20 minutes
Serve: 6

Ingredients:

- 1 lb pork, boneless and cut into bite-sized pieces
- ¼ tsp paprika
- ½ tsp garlic powder
- ½ tsp onion powder
- ¼ tsp pepper
- ¼ tsp sea salt
- For marinade:
- ½ tsp ground ginger
- 1 tbsp fresh lime juice
- 1/3 cup olive oil
- 2/3 cup coconut amino
- ½ tsp pepper
- ½ tsp sea salt

Directions:

1. Add all marinade ingredients into the mixing bowl and mix well.
2. Add meat to the bowl and coat well with marinade and place in the refrigerator for 30 minutes.
3. Preheat the oven to 350 F.
4. Arrange marinated meat pieces on a baking tray and cook in preheated oven for 10 minutes. Turn meat pieces to another side and cook for 10 minutes more.
5. Serve and enjoy.

Nutritional Value (Amount per Serving):

- Calories 234

- Fat 13.9 g
- Carbohydrates 6 g
- Sugar 0.2 g
- Protein 19.9 g
- Cholesterol 55 mg

Shredded Cilantro Lime Pork

Preparation Time: 10 minutes
Cooking Time: 6 hours
Serve: 6

Ingredients:

- 2 lbs pork sirloin roast
- ¼ tsp garlic powder
- ¼ cup fresh cilantro, chopped
- ½ tbsp cumin
- 1 ½ tbsp chili powder
- ¼ cup fresh lime juice
- 1 ½ tsp kosher salt

Directions:

1. Place pork into the slow cooker.
2. Add remaining ingredients on top of the pork.
3. Cover slow cooker with lid and cook on low for 6 hours.
4. Remove pork from slow cooker and shred using a fork.
5. Return shredded pork to the slow cooker and stir well.
6. Serve and enjoy.

Nutritional Value (Amount per Serving):

- Calories 321
- Fat 14.7g
- Carbohydrates 1.3 g
- Sugar 0.2 g
- Protein 43.4 g
- Cholesterol 130 mg

Grilled Lamb Chops

Preparation Time: 10 minutes
Cooking Time: 10 minutes
Serve: 6

Ingredients:

- 2 lbs lamb chops
- ¼ cup olive oil
- 1 lemon zest
- ½ tsp black pepper
- 1 tbsp fresh rosemary, chopped
- 1 tbsp garlic, minced
- 1 ¼ tsp kosher salt

Directions:

1. In a mixing bowl, mix together garlic, oil, lemon zest, rosemary, pepper, and salt.
2. Place lamb chops in a bowl and coat with marinade and place in the refrigerator for 1 hour.
3. Heat grill over medium-high heat.
4. Place marinated lamb chops on hot grill and sear for 2-3 minutes on each side.
5. Turn heat to medium and cook for 5-6 minutes or until internal temperature reaches 150 F.
6. Serve and enjoy.

Nutritional Value (Amount per Serving):

- Calories 358
- Fat 19.6 g
- Carbohydrates 0.9 g
- Sugar 0 g
- Protein 42.6 g
- Cholesterol 136 mg

Pork Tacos

Preparation Time: 10 minutes
Cooking Time: 8 hours
Serve: 8

Ingredients:

- 2 lbs pork tenderloin
- 23.5 oz salsa
- 2 1/2 tsp garlic powder
- 1 1/2 tbsp ground cumin
- 2 tbsp chili powder
- 1 1/2 tsp cayenne pepper
- 1 1/2 tsp salt

Directions:

1. Place pork in the slow cooker.
2. In a small bowl, mix together all remaining ingredients except salsa.
3. Rub spice mixture over pork. Pour salsa on top of the pork.
4. Cover slow cooker with lid and cook on low for 8 hours.
5. Remove meat from slow cooker and shred using a fork.
6. Return shredded meat into the slow cooker and stir well.
7. Serve and enjoy.

Nutritional Value (Amount per Serving):

- Calories 201
- Fat 4 g
- Carbohydrates 7.5 g
- Sugar 3 g
- Protein 30 g
- Cholesterol 83 mg

Italian Lamb Chops

Preparation Time: 10 minutes
Cooking Time: 15 minutes
Serve: 4

Ingredients:

- 8 lamb chops
- 2 tbsp olive oil
- 2 tbsp Dijon mustard
- 1 1/2 tsp Italian seasoning
- 1 tsp garlic, minced
- Pepper
- Salt

Directions:

1. Preheat the oven to 425 F.
2. Season pork chops with pepper and salt and place on a baking tray.
3. In a small bowl, mix together the remaining ingredients and spoon over each pork chops and spread well.
4. Bake for 15 minutes.
5. Serve and enjoy.

Nutritional Value (Amount per Serving):

- Calories 391
- Fat 21.2 g
- Carbohydrates 1 g
- Sugar 0.5 g
- Protein 48 g
- Cholesterol 150 mg

Pork Stir Fry

Preparation Time: 10 minutes
Cooking Time: 15 minutes
Serve: 4

Ingredients:

- 1 lb ground pork
- 1 1/2 tsp red chili sauce
- 1 tbsp soy sauce, low-sodium
- 3 garlic cloves, minced
- 1/2 cup cilantro, chopped
- 1/4 cup green onion, chopped
- 2 jalapeno pepper, chopped
- 1 tbsp fresh lemon juice
- 1 tbsp ginger, minced
- 2 tbsp sesame oil
- 1 tbsp olive oil

Directions:

1. Heat oil in a pan over medium heat.
2. Add garlic and ginger and sauté for a minute.
3. Add pork and cook until browned.
4. Once the meat is cooked then add remaining ingredients and stir well.
5. Serve and enjoy.

Nutritional Value (Amount per Serving):

- Calories 415
- Fat 31 g
- Carbohydrates 3 g
- Sugar 1 g
- Protein 20 g
- Cholesterol 121 mg

Meatballs

Preparation Time: 10 minutes
Cooking Time: 20 minutes
Serve: 12

Ingredients:

- 1 egg
- 1 lb ground beef
- 1 lb ground pork
- 1/2 tsp garlic powder
- 2 tbsp onion, chopped
- 1/3 cup coconut milk
- 1/4 cup parmesan cheese, shredded
- 1/4 cup fresh parsley, chopped
- 1 tsp Italian seasoning
- 1/4 cup almond flour
- Pepper
- Salt

Directions:

1. Preheat the oven to 400 F.
2. Add all ingredients into the large bowl and mix until well combined.
3. Make small balls from the meat mixture and place them on a baking tray.
4. Bake for 20 minutes.
5. Serve and enjoy.

Nutritional Value (Amount per Serving):

- Calories 192
- Fat 7 g
- Carbohydrates 4 g
- Sugar 0.7 g
- Protein 24 g
- Cholesterol 80 mg

Easy Pork Tenderloin

Preparation Time: 10 minutes
Cooking Time: 30 minutes
Serve: 6

Ingredients:

- 2 lbs pork tenderloin
- For rub:
- 1 tbsp garlic powder
- 1 tbsp onion powder
- 1 tbsp paprika
- 1/2 tbsp salt

Directions:

1. Preheat the oven to 425 F.
2. In a small bowl, mix together all rub ingredients and rub over pork.
3. Spray pan with cooking spray and heat over medium-high heat.
4. Sear pork on all sides until lightly golden brown.
5. Place into the preheated oven and roast for about 25-30 minutes.
6. Slice and serve.

Nutritional Value (Amount per Serving):

- Calories 228
- Fat 5.5 g
- Carbohydrates 2.6 g
- Sugar 0.9 g
- Protein 40.1 g
- Cholesterol 110 mg

Chapter 8: Poultry

Chicken Avocado Salad

Preparation Time: 10 minutes
Cooking Time: 10 minutes
Serve: 3

Ingredients:

- 2 chicken breasts, cooked and cubed
- 1 tbsp fresh lime juice
- 2 avocados, peeled and pitted
- 2 Serrano chili peppers, chopped
- 1/4 cup celery, chopped
- 1 onion, chopped
- 1 cup cilantro, chopped
- 1 tsp kosher salt

Directions:

1. Scoop out avocados flesh using a spoon and place it into the bowl.
2. Mash the avocado flesh using a fork.
3. Add remaining ingredients and mix until well combined.
4. Serve and enjoy.

Nutritional Value (Amount per Serving):

- Calories 236
- Fat 10.6 g
- Carbohydrates 4.5 g
- Sugar 1 g
- Protein 29 g
- Cholesterol 87 mg

Paprika Chicken

Preparation Time: 10 minutes
Cooking Time: 35 minutes
Serve: 4

Ingredients:

- 4 chicken breasts, skinless and boneless, cut into chunks
- 2 tbsp paprika
- 2 1/2 tbsp olive oil
- 1 1/2 tsp garlic, minced
- 2 tbsp fresh lemon juice
- Pepper
- Salt

Directions:

1. Preheat the oven to 350 F.
2. In a small bowl, mix together garlic, lemon juice, paprika, and olive oil.
3. Season chicken with pepper and salt.
4. Spread 1/3 bowl mixture on the bottom of the casserole dish.
5. Add chicken into the casserole dish and rub with dish sauce.
6. Pour remaining sauce over chicken and rub well.
7. Bake for 30-35 minutes.
8. Serve and enjoy.

Nutritional Value (Amount per Serving):

- Calories 380
- Fat 22 g
- Carbohydrates 2.6 g
- Sugar 0.5 g
- Protein 43 g
- Cholesterol 130 mg

Parmesan Chicken

Preparation Time: 10 minutes
Cooking Time: 35 minutes
Serve: 4

Ingredients:

- 1 lb chicken breasts, skinless and boneless
- 1/2 cup parmesan cheese, grated
- 3/4 cup mayonnaise
- 1 tsp garlic powder
- 1/2 tsp Italian seasoning

Directions:

1. Preheat the oven to 375 F.
2. Spray baking dish with cooking spray.
3. In a small bowl, mix together mayonnaise, garlic powder, poultry seasoning, and pepper.
4. Place chicken breasts into the prepared baking dish.
5. Spread mayonnaise mixture over chicken then sprinkles cheese on top of chicken.
6. Bake chicken for 35 minutes.
7. Serve and enjoy.

Nutritional Value (Amount per Serving):

- Calories 391
- Fat 23 g
- Carbohydrates 11 g
- Sugar 3 g
- Protein 33 g
- Cholesterol 112 mg

Delicious Chicken Wings

Preparation Time: 10 minutes
Cooking Time: 30 minutes
Serve: 6

Ingredients:

- 1 egg, beaten
- 1 1/2 lbs chicken wings
- 6 tbsp olive oil
- 1/2 cup apple cider vinegar
- 1/2 tsp cayenne pepper
- 2 garlic cloves, minced
- 1/2 tsp pepper
- 3/4 tsp salt

Directions:

1. Add all ingredients except chicken in a large bowl and mix well.
2. Add chicken wings in a bowl and mix until well coated and set aside for 20 minutes.
3. Preheat the oven to 450 F.
4. Spray a baking tray with cooking spray.
5. Place marinated wings on a prepared baking tray and bake for 30 minutes.
6. Serve and enjoy.

Nutritional Value (Amount per Serving):

- Calories 355
- Fat 23 g
- Carbohydrates 0.5 g
- Sugar 0.1 g
- Protein 33 g
- Cholesterol 128 mg

Lemon Chicken

Preparation Time: 10 minutes
Cooking Time: 45 minutes
Serve: 8

Ingredients:

- 8 chicken breasts, skinless and boneless
- 1/4 cup fresh lemon juice
- 2 tbsp green onion, chopped
- 1 tbsp oregano leaves
- 3 oz feta cheese, crumbled
- 1/4 tsp pepper

Directions:

1. Preheat the oven to 350 F.
2. Spray baking dish with cooking spray.
3. Place chicken breasts in prepared baking dish.
4. Drizzle with 2 tbsp lemon juice and sprinkle with 1/2 tablespoon oregano and pepper.
5. Top with green onion and crumbled cheese.
6. Drizzle with remaining lemon juice and oregano.
7. Bake for 45 minutes.
8. Serve and enjoy.

Nutritional Value (Amount per Serving):

- Calories 246
- Fat 10.8 g
- Carbohydrates 1.2 g
- Sugar 0.5 g
- Protein 34 g
- Cholesterol 110 mg

Yummy Chicken Skewers

Preparation Time: 10 minutes
Cooking Time: 10 minutes
Serve: 8

Ingredients:

- 2 lbs chicken breast tenderloins
- 1 tsp lemon pepper seasoning
- 1 tsp garlic, minced
- 1 tbsp olive oil
- 1 cup of salsa

Directions:

1. Add chicken in a zip-lock bag along with 1/4 cup salsa, lemon pepper seasoning, garlic, and oil.
2. Seal bag and shake well and place it in the refrigerator overnight.
3. Thread marinated chicken onto the soaked wooden skewers.
4. Place skewers on hot grill and cooks for 8-10 minutes.
5. Brush with remaining salsa during the last 3 minutes of grilling.
6. Serve and enjoy.

Nutritional Value (Amount per Serving):

- Calories 125
- Fat 2.5 g
- Carbohydrates 2.1 g
- Sugar 1 g
- Protein 24 g
- Cholesterol 71 mg

Tasty Shredded Chicken

Preparation Time: 10 minutes
Cooking Time: 25 minutes
Serve: 6

Ingredients:

- 3 chicken breast, boneless and skinless
- 1/4 cup vinegar
- 13.5 oz chunky salsa
- 1/4 tsp onion powder
- 1 tbsp ground cumin
- 1 1/2 tbsp chili powder

Directions:

1. Add all ingredients into the instant pot and stir well.
2. Seal pot with lid and cook on manual high pressure for 25 minutes.
3. Once done, then release pressure using the quick-release method than open the lid.
4. Remove chicken from pot and shred using a fork.
5. Serve and enjoy.

Nutritional Value (Amount per Serving):

- Calories 171
- Fat 6.3 g
- Carbohydrates 5 g
- Sugar 2.2 g
- Protein 23 g
- Cholesterol 64 mg

Flavorful Herb Chicken

Preparation Time: 10 minutes
Cooking Time: 15 minutes
Serve: 5

Ingredients:

- 2 lbs chicken breast, skinless and boneless
- 1/2 cup Greek yogurt
- 1/4 cup mayonnaise
- 1 1/2 tsp herb seasoning
- 1/2 tsp onion powder
- 1/2 tsp garlic powder
- 1/4 tsp salt

Directions:

1. Preheat the air-fryer to 380 F.
2. In a small bowl, mix together mayonnaise, herb seasoning, onion powder, garlic powder, and yogurt.
3. Coat chicken with mayo mixture.
4. Spray air-fryer basket with cooking spray.
5. Place chicken in an air-fryer basket and cook for 15 minutes. Turn halfway through.
6. Serve and enjoy.

Nutritional Value (Amount per Serving):

- Calories 272
- Fat 8 g
- Carbohydrates 5 g
- Sugar 2 g
- Protein 40 g
- Cholesterol 121 mg

Tasty Shredded Chicken

Preparation Time: 10 minutes
Cooking Time: 15 minutes
Serve: 4

Ingredients:

- 1 1/2 lbs chicken breast, skinless and boneless
- 1 tsp onion powder
- 1 tsp garlic powder
- 2 cups chicken broth
- 1/2 tsp oregano
- 1/2 tsp cumin
- 1 tsp chili powder
- Pepper
- Salt

Directions:

1. In a small bowl, mix together onion powder, garlic powder, oregano, cumin, chili powder, and salt.
2. Coat chicken with spice mixture and place in a large pot.
3. Pour broth over the chicken and bring to boil.
4. Once it begins to boiling then turn heat to low and simmer for 10 minutes or until chicken is cooked.
5. Remove chicken from pot and shred using a fork.
6. Return shredded chicken to the pot and stir well and simmer for 5 minutes more.
7. Serve and enjoy.

Nutritional Value (Amount per Serving):

- Calories 220
- Fat 5 g
- Carbohydrates 2.1 g
- Sugar 1 g
- Protein 39 g
- Cholesterol 109 mg

Chicken Bacon Salad

Preparation Time: 10 minutes
Cooking Time: 10 minutes
Serve: 4

Ingredients:

- 2 chicken breasts, cooked and chopped
- 3 bacon slices, cooked and chopped
- 1/2 cup celery, diced
- 2 avocado, chopped
- 2 1/2 tbsp olive oil
- 3 tbsp fresh lemon juice
- 1/2 tsp dried dill
- 1 tbsp dried chives
- 1/2 tsp pepper
- 1 tsp salt

Directions:

1. Add all ingredients into the large bowl and toss well to combine.
2. Serve and enjoy.

Nutritional Value (Amount per Serving):

- Calories 441
- Fat 36 g
- Carbohydrates 10 g
- Sugar 1 g
- Protein 24 g
- Cholesterol 66 mg

Chapter 9: Seafood

Grilled Mahi Mahi

Preparation Time: 10 minutes
Cooking Time: 10 minutes
Serve: 6

Ingredients:

- 6 mahi-mahi fillets
- ¼ cup chicken stock
- ½ tsp garlic, minced
- 1 small onion, minced
- 6 tbsp butter
- 2 tbsp olive oil
- 2 tbsp lemon juice

Directions:

1. Preheat the grill to medium-high heat.
2. Place fish fillets in a mixing bowl. Add oil, pepper, and salt over fish fillets and coat well.
3. Place fish on hot grill and cook for 3-4 minutes on each side.
4. Transfer fish to a serving dish.
5. Melt 1 tbsp of butter in a pan over medium-high heat.
6. Add onion and sauté for 2 minutes or until onion is softened.
7. Add garlic and sauté for a minute.
8. Add stock and simmer until liquid reduced by half.
9. Add lemon juice and cook for a minute.
10. Remove pan from heat and add remaining butter and stir until sauce thickens.
11. Pour sauce over grilled fish and serve.

Nutritional Value (Amount per Serving):

- Calories 237
- Fat 16.2 g
- Carbohydrates 1.2 g
- Sugar 0.5 g
- Protein 21.3 g
- Cholesterol 71 mg

Crab Salad

Preparation Time: 10 minutes
Cooking Time: 10 minutes
Serve: 6

Ingredients:

- 8 oz crab meat
- 2 celery stalks, sliced
- ½ tsp Worcestershire sauce
- ½ tsp old bay spice
- ½ tsp dried dill
- 1 tsp lemon juice
- 2 tbsp fresh parsley, chopped
- ¼ cup mayonnaise
- ½ cup sour cream
- 4 oz cream cheese
- 1 tbsp garlic, crushed
- ¼ cup onion, diced
- 2 tbsp butter

Directions:

1. Melt butter in a small pan over medium heat.
2. Add onion and sauté until softened.
3. Add garlic and sauté for a minute.
4. Transfer onion-garlic mixture to the large bowl.
5. Add remaining ingredients to the bowl and stir everything well to combine.
6. Serve and enjoy.

Nutritional Value (Amount per Serving):

- Calories 219
- Fat 18.4 g

- Carbohydrates 5.6 g
- Sugar 1.1 g
- Protein 7.2 g
- Cholesterol 62 mg

Garlic Shrimp

Preparation Time: 10 minutes
Cooking Time: 10 minutes
Serve: 4

Ingredients:

- 1 lb shrimp
- 2 tbsp fresh parsley, chopped
- ½ cup parmesan cheese, grated
- 1 ½ cups heavy cream
- ½ cup chicken stock
- 5 garlic cloves, minced
- 2 tbsp butter
- 1 tbsp olive oil
- Pepper
- Salt

Directions:

1. Heat olive oil in a large pan over medium-high heat.
2. Add shrimp to the pan and season with pepper and salt and cook shrimp for 1-2 minutes on each side.
3. Transfer shrimp to the bowl and set aside.
4. Melt butter in the same pan. Add garlic and sauté for a minute.
5. Add stock and cook until stock reduced by half.
6. Turn heat to medium-low. Add cream and stir well and simmer for 2-3 minutes.
7. Add cheese and cook until cheese is melted.
8. Return shrimp to the pan.
9. Garnish with parsley and serve.

Nutritional Value (Amount per Serving):

- Calories 453

- Fat 32.4 g
- Carbohydrates 4.5 g
- Sugar 0.2 g
- Protein 33.2 g
- Cholesterol 331 mg

Easy Seafood Salad

Preparation Time: 10 minutes
Cooking Time: 3 minutes
Serve: 4

Ingredients:

- 8 oz shrimp
- 8 oz crab meat
- 1 tbsp dill, chopped
- ½ cup mayonnaise
- 2 tsp lemon juice
- ¼ tsp old bay seasoning
- ¼ cup onion, minced
- ½ cup celery, chopped
- 1 lemon, quartered
- Pepper
- Salt

Directions:

1. Add lemon and water to the pot and bring to boil.
2. Add shrimp to the pot and cook for 1-2 minutes.
3. Drain shrimp well and place it in a large bowl.
4. Add remaining ingredients to the bowl and stir until well combined.
5. Cover salad bowl and place in the refrigerator for 2 hours.
6. Serve chilled and enjoy.

Nutritional Value (Amount per Serving):

- Calories 240
- Fat 11 g
- Carbohydrates 10 g
- Sugar 2.4 g
- Protein 20.6 g
- Cholesterol 157 mg

Easy Crab Cakes

Preparation Time: 10 minutes
Cooking Time: 10 minutes
Serve: 2

Ingredients:

- 8 oz crab meat
- 2 tbsp butter
- ¼ tsp pepper
- ½ tsp old bay seasoning
- 2 tbsp mayonnaise
- 1 egg, lightly beaten
- ¼ cup almond flour
- ¼ cup red pepper, diced
- 1 small onion, diced

Directions:

1. Add all ingredients except butter in a mixing bowl and mix until well combined.
2. Make small patties from bowl mixture.
3. Melt butter in a pan over medium heat.
4. Fry crab cakes for 2-3 minutes on each side or until lightly golden brown.
5. Serve and enjoy.

Nutritional Value (Amount per Serving):

- Calories 311
- Fat 20.7 g
- Carbohydrates 10.3 g
- Sugar 3.4 g
- Protein 17.8 g
- Cholesterol 177 mg

Nutritious Tuna Patties

Preparation Time: 10 minutes
Cooking Time: 15 minutes
Serve: 8

Ingredients:

- 2 cans tuna, drained and flaked
- 4 tbsp olive oil
- ¼ cup fresh parsley, chopped
- 2 eggs, lightly beaten
- 3 garlic cloves, minced
- 2 tbsp Dijon mustard
- 2 tbsp mayonnaise
- ¼ tsp pepper
- ½ tsp salt

Directions:

1. Preheat the oven to 170 F.
2. In a bowl, mix together tuna, parsley, eggs, garlic, Dijon mustard, mayonnaise, pepper, and salt.
3. Heat oil in a pan over medium heat.
4. Make small patties from tuna mixture and fry until golden brown, about 2-3 minutes per side.
5. Serve and enjoy.

Nutritional Value (Amount per Serving):

- Calories 178
- Fat 13.1 g
- Carbohydrates 1.7 g
- Sugar 0.4 g
- Protein 13.5 g
- Cholesterol 56 mg

Quick Butter Cod

Preparation Time: 10 minutes
Cooking Time: 5 minutes
Serve: 4

Ingredients:

- 1 ½ lbs cod fillets, cut into pieces
- ½ tsp paprika
- ¼ tsp ground pepper
- ¼ tsp garlic powder
- 6 tbsp butter
- ½ tsp salt

Directions:

1. In a small bowl, mix together paprika, pepper, garlic powder, and salt.
2. Coat fish pieces with seasoning mixture.
3. Melt 2 tbsp of butter in a large pan over medium-high heat.
4. Add fish pieces to the pan and cook for 2 minutes.
5. Turn heat to medium. Add remaining butter on top of fish pieces and cook for 3-4 minutes.
6. Once fish is cooked completely then remove the pan from heat.
7. Add lemon juice and stir well.
8. Serve and enjoy.

Nutritional Value (Amount per Serving):

- Calories 291
- Fat 18.8 g
- Carbohydrates 0.4 g
- Sugar 0.1 g
- Protein 30.6 g
- Cholesterol 129 mg

Baked Tilapia

Preparation Time: 10 minutes
Cooking Time: 10 minutes
Serve: 4

Ingredients:

- 4 tilapia fillets
- 1 lemon zest
- 2 tbsp fresh lemon juice
- 1 tbsp garlic, minced
- ¼ cup butter, melted
- 2 tbsp fresh parsley, chopped
- Pepper
- Salt

Directions:

1. Preheat the oven to 425 F.
2. In a small bowl, mix together butter, lemon zest, lemon juice, and garlic and set aside.
3. Season fish fillets with pepper and salt.
4. Place fish fillets onto the baking dish. Pour butter mixture over fish fillets.
5. Bake fish in preheated oven for 10-12 minutes.
6. Garnish with parsley and serve.

Nutritional Value (Amount per Serving):

- Calories 247
- Fat 13.6 g
- Carbohydrates 1 g
- Sugar 0.2 g
- Protein 32.4 g
- Cholesterol 116 mg

Shrimp Avocado Salad

Preparation Time: 10 minutes
Cooking Time: 5 minutes
Serve: 4

Ingredients:

- 16 oz shrimp, thawed and drained
- 1 avocado, pitted and diced
- ¼ cup celery, chopped
- 1 small onion, chopped
- 2 ½ tbsp fresh dill, chopped
- 1 tbsp vinegar
- 1 tsp Dijon mustard
- ½ cup mayonnaise
- Pepper
- Salt

Directions:

1. In a small bowl, mix together mayonnaise, dill, vinegar, and mustard. Set aside.
2. Add shrimp, onion, and celery in a mixing bowl.
3. Pour mayonnaise mixture over shrimp and stir well.
4. Cover and place in the refrigerator for 1-2 hours.
5. Add avocado and serve immediately.

Nutritional Value (Amount per Serving):

- Calories 279
- Fat 13.1 g
- Carbohydrates 12.5 g
- Sugar 2.7 g
- Protein 27 g
- Cholesterol 246 mg

Paprika Shrimp

Preparation Time: 10 minutes
Cooking Time: 50 minutes
Serve: 8

Ingredients:

- 2 lbs shrimp, peeled and deveined
- 1 tsp paprika
- 5 garlic cloves, sliced
- 3/4 cup olive oil
- 1/2 tsp red pepper flakes, crushed
- 1/4 tsp pepper
- 1 tsp kosher salt

Directions:

1. Add oil, red pepper flakes, pepper, paprika, garlic, and salt into the slow cooker and stir well.
2. Cover and cook on high for 30 minutes.
3. Add shrimp. Stir and cook for 10 minutes.
4. Cover again and cook for 10 minutes more.
5. Serve and enjoy.

Nutritional Value (Amount per Serving):

- Calories 300
- Fat 20.2 g
- Carbohydrates 2.7 g
- Sugar 0.3 g
- Protein 25 g
- Cholesterol 240 mg

Chapter 10: Soups & Sides

Creamy Asparagus Soup

Preparation Time: 10 minutes
Cooking Time: 15 minutes
Serve: 6

Ingredients:

- 2 lbs asparagus, cut the ends and chop into ½-inch pieces
- 2 tbsp olive oil
- 3 garlic cloves, minced
- 2 oz parmesan cheese, grated
- ½ cup heavy cream
- ¼ cup onion, chopped
- 4 cups vegetable stock
- Pepper
- Salt

Directions:

1. Heat olive oil in a large pot over medium heat.
2. Add onion to the pot and sauté until onion is softened.
3. Add asparagus and sauté for 2-3 minutes.
4. Add garlic and sauté for a minute. Season with pepper and salt.
5. Add stock and bring to boil. Turn heat to low and simmer until asparagus is tender.
6. Remove pot from heat and puree the soup using an immersion blender until creamy.
7. Return pot on heat. Add cream and stir well and cook over medium heat until just soup is hot. Do not boil the soup.
8. Remove from heat. Add cheese and stir well.
9. Serve and enjoy.

Nutritional Value (Amount per Serving):

- Calories 146
- Fat 11.9 g
- Carbohydrates 8.8 g
- Sugar 4.4 g
- Protein 6.7 g
- Cholesterol 20 mg

Healthy Celery Soup

Preparation Time: 10 minutes
Cooking Time: 20 minutes
Serve: 4

Ingredients:

- 3 cups celery, chopped
- 1 cup vegetable broth
- 5 oz cream cheese
- 1 ½ tbsp fresh basil, chopped
- ¼ cup onion, chopped
- 1 tbsp garlic, chopped
- 1 tbsp olive oil
- ¼ tsp pepper
- ½ tsp salt

Directions:

1. Heat oil in a large saucepan over medium heat.
2. Add onion, garlic, and celery to the saucepan and sauté for 4-5 minutes or until softened.
3. Add broth and bring to boil. Turn heat to low and simmer.
4. Add basil and cream cheese and stir until cheese is melted.
5. Season soup with pepper and salt.
6. Remove from heat and puree the soup using an immersion blender until smooth and creamy.
7. Serve and enjoy.

Nutritional Value (Amount per Serving):

- Calories 182
- Fat 16.4 g
- Carbohydrates 4.9 g
- Sugar 1.6 g
- Protein 4.7 g
- Cholesterol 39 mg

Flavorful Cauliflower Soup

Preparation Time: 10 minutes
Cooking Time: 25 minutes
Serve: 6

Ingredients:

- 3 cups cauliflower florets
- 3.5 oz cream cheese
- ½ cup heavy cream
- 3 cups vegetable stock
- ½ tbsp fresh thyme, chopped
- 1 tbsp garlic, minced
- 2 tbsp olive oil
- 2 tbsp butter
- ¼ tsp pepper
- ¼ tsp salt

Directions:

1. Preheat the oven to 425 F.
2. Spread cauliflower florets onto the baking tray and drizzle with oil. Season with pepper and salt.
3. Roast cauliflower in preheated oven for 10-15 minutes and set aside.
4. Melt butter in large pot over medium heat.
5. Add thyme and garlic and sauté for a minute.
6. Add cream, cream cheese, and stock and stir well. Simmer over medium heat until cheese is melted.
7. Add roasted cauliflower and bring to boil. Turn heat to low and simmer for 10 minutes.
8. Remove pot from heat and puree the soup using an immersion blender until smooth.
9. Serve and enjoy.

Nutritional Value (Amount per Serving):

- Calories 187
- Fat 19.1 g
- Carbohydrates 5 g
- Sugar 2.3 g
- Protein 2.6 g
- Cholesterol 42 mg

Basil Zucchini Soup

Preparation Time: 10 minutes
Cooking Time: 25 minutes
Serve: 4

Ingredients:

- 2 medium zucchinis, chopped
- ¼ cup fresh basil leaves
- 3 cups vegetable broth
- 3 tbsp olive oil
- 1 tbsp garlic, chopped
- 1 medium onion, chopped
- ¼ tsp pepper
- ½ tsp salt

Directions:

1. Heat olive oil in a saucepan over medium heat.
2. Add garlic and onion and sauté for 3-5 minutes or until onion is softened.
3. Add zucchini and cook for 5 minutes.
4. Add stock and bring to boil. Turn heat to low and simmer for 15 minutes.
5. Remove from heat. Add basil and stir well.
6. Puree the soup using an immersion blender until smooth.
7. Season soup with pepper and salt.
8. Serve and enjoy.

Nutritional Value (Amount per Serving):

- Calories 149
- Fat 11.8 g
- Carbohydrates 7.3 g
- Sugar 3.4 g
- Protein 5.3 g

Warm & Delicious Chicken Soup

Preparation Time: 10 minutes
Cooking Time: 20 minutes
Serve: 4

Ingredients:

- 4 chicken thighs, skinless, deboned, cooked and chopped
- 2 tbsp fresh parsley, chopped
- 2 celery ribs, chopped
- 3 cups chicken stock
- ½ cup heavy cream
- ½ cup of coconut milk
- 1/3 cup water
- 3 oz mushrooms, sliced
- 1 tbsp garlic, chopped
- 2 tbsp butter
- 3 bacon slices, cooked and chopped
- Pepper
- Salt

Directions:

1. Melt butter in a large pot over medium heat.
2. Add mushrooms and garlic and cook until mushrooms are softened.
3. Add water and cook until water reduced by half.
4. Stir in stock, heavy cream, and coconut milk.
5. Add chicken and celery. Stir well and simmer until just soup is hot. Do not boil the soup.
6. Season soup with pepper and salt.
7. Garnish with bacon and parsley.
8. Serve and enjoy.

Nutritional Value (Amount per Serving):

- Calories 543
- Fat 35.8 g
- Carbohydrates 4.6 g
- Sugar 2.1 g
- Protein 50 g
- Cholesterol 181 mg

Creamy Mushroom Soup

Preparation Time: 10 minutes
Cooking Time: 40 minutes
Serve: 4

Ingredients:

- 1 lb mushroom, washed and sliced
- ½ cup heavy cream
- ½ tsp dried thyme
- 4 cups vegetable stock
- 3 tbsp butter
- ¼ cup onion, chopped
- Pepper
- Salt

Directions:

1. Melt butter in a large pot over medium heat.
2. Add onion and sauté for 2-3 minutes.
3. Add mushrooms and cook for 4-5 minutes.
4. Add thyme and stock and stir well. Cover pot with lid and simmer for 30 minutes.
5. Remove from heat and puree the soup using blender until smooth.
6. Add heavy cream and stir well. Season soup with pepper and salt.
7. Serve and enjoy.

Nutritional Value (Amount per Serving):

- Calories 158
- Fat 15 g
- Carbohydrates 5.4 g
- Sugar 2.8 g
- Protein 4.1 g
- Cholesterol 43 mg

Flavorful Kale Cauliflower Soup

Preparation Time: 10 minutes
Cooking Time: 1 hour 20 minutes
Serve: 4

Ingredients:

- 4 cups cauliflower florets
- 6 cups vegetable stock
- 1 tbsp garlic, minced
- ¼ cup onion, chopped
- 6 oz kale, chopped
- 6 tbsp olive oil
- Pepper
- Salt

Directions:

1. Preheat the oven to 425 F.
2. Spread cauliflower onto the baking tray and drizzle with 2 tablespoons of oil and season with pepper and salt.
3. Roast cauliflower in preheated oven for 25 minutes. Remove from the oven and set aside.
4. In a bowl, toss kale with 2 tablespoons of oil and season with salt. Arrange kale onto the baking tray and bake at 300 F for 30 minutes. Toss halfway through.
5. Heat remaining oil in a large saucepan over medium heat.
6. Add onion and sauté for 3-4 minutes. Add garlic and sauté for a minute.
7. Add stock and roasted cauliflower and bring to boil.
8. Turn heat to low and simmer for 10 minutes.
9. Add kale and cook for 10 minutes more.
10. Remove from heat and puree the soup using an immersion blender until smooth.
11. Serve and enjoy.

Nutritional Value (Amount per Serving):

- Calories 235
- Fat 21.6 g
- Carbohydrates 11.6 g
- Sugar 3.2 g
- Protein 3.5 g
- Cholesterol 0 mg

Delicious Pumpkin Soup

Preparation Time: 10 minutes
Cooking Time: 15 minutes
Serve: 6

Ingredients:

- 14.5 oz pumpkin puree
- ½ cup heavy cream
- 2 tbsp fresh parsley, chopped
- ½ tsp fresh thyme, chopped
- ½ tsp garlic powder
- 4 cups vegetable stock
- ¼ tsp pepper
- ½ tsp salt

Directions:

1. Add all ingredients except heavy cream into the saucepan and stir to combine. Bring to boil over medium-high heat.
2. Turn heat to low and simmer for 10 minutes.
3. Remove from heat. Add heavy cream and stir well.
4. Garnish with parsley and serve.

Nutritional Value (Amount per Serving):

- Calories 61
- Fat 4.2 g
- Carbohydrates 6.4 g
- Sugar 2.7 g
- Protein 1 g
- Cholesterol 14 mg

Chicken Cauliflower Soup

Preparation Time: 10 minutes
Cooking Time: 10 minutes
Serve: 4

Ingredients:

- 2 cups chicken, cooked and shredded
- 4 oz cream cheese, cubed
- 1 tbsp garlic, minced
- 2 tbsp butter
- 1 ½ cup cauliflower rice, cooked
- ½ tsp onion powder
- ¼ cup heavy cream
- 14.5 oz chicken stock
- Salt

Directions:

1. Melt butter in a medium saucepan over medium heat.
2. Add garlic and sauté for a minute. Add chicken and stir well.
3. Add cream cheese and stir until cheese is melted.
4. Add stock, onion powder, heavy cream, and salt. Stir well and bring to boil over medium-high heat.
5. Turn heat to low and simmer for 3-4 minutes.
6. Stir in cauliflower rice and cook for 2-3 minutes.
7. Serve and enjoy.

Nutritional Value (Amount per Serving):

- Calories 299
- Fat 20.8 g
- Carbohydrates 4.2 g
- Sugar 1.4 g
- Protein 23.8 g
- Cholesterol 111 mg

Creamy Cauliflower Mashed

Preparation Time: 10 minutes

Cooking Time: 10 minutes

Serve: 6

Ingredients:

- 1 large cauliflower head, cut into florets
- 1 tbsp fresh parsley, chopped
- ¼ tsp paprika
- 1 tsp onion powder
- 2 tbsp butter
- 1/3 cup coconut cream
- Pepper
- Salt

Directions:

1. Add cauliflower florets and 2 tbsp water into the microwave-safe bowl. Cover and microwave for 5 minutes.
2. Stir cauliflower and microwave for 5 minutes more.
3. Drain cauliflower well and place in a food processor. Add remaining ingredients except for parsley and process until smooth and creamy.
4. Garnish with parsley and serve.

Nutritional Value (Amount per Serving):

- Calories 102
- Fat 7.2 g
- Carbohydrates 8.6 g
- Sugar 4 g
- Protein 3.2 g
- Cholesterol 10 mg

Chapter 11: Desserts

Mug Cake

Preparation Time: 5 minutes
Cooking Time: 2 minutes
Serve: 1

Ingredients:

- 1 egg, lightly beaten
- 1/8 tsp baking powder, gluten-free
- 2 tbsp creamy peanut butter
- 1 tbsp Swerve

Directions:

1. Add all ingredients into the microwave-safe mug and stir until well combined.
2. Place mug in microwave and microwave for 1-2 minutes.
3. Serve and enjoy.

Nutritional Value (Amount per Serving):

- Calories 257
- Fat 20.5 g
- Carbohydrates 8.9 g
- Sugar 3.3 g
- Protein 13.5 g
- Cholesterol 164 mg

Chocó Fat Bombs

Preparation Time: 10 minutes
Cooking Time: 5 minutes
Serve: 30

Ingredients:

- 3.5 oz unsweetened dark chocolate
- 6 drops liquid stevia
- ¼ cup of coconut oil

Directions:

1. Add chocolate, oil, and sweetener in microwave-safe bowl and microwave until chocolate is melted.
2. Pour chocolate mixture into the mold and place it in the refrigerator until set.
3. Serve and enjoy.

Nutritional Value (Amount per Serving):

- Calories 38
- Fat 3.6 g
- Carbohydrates 0.9 g
- Sugar 0 g
- Protein 0.4 g
- Cholesterol 0 mg

Delicious Chocolate Frosty

Preparation Time: 10 minutes
Cooking Time: 10 minutes
Serve: 2

Ingredients:

- 1 ½ cups heavy whipping cream
- 2 ½ tbsp lakanto monk fruit
- 1 tbsp vanilla
- 2 tbsp unsweetened cocoa powder

Directions:

1. Add all ingredients into the large mixing bowl.
2. Beat using the hand mixer until peaks form.
3. Scoop mixture into the zip-lock bag and place it in the refrigerator for 45 minutes.
4. Remove a zip-lock bag from the refrigerator and cut the corner of the bag.
5. Squeeze frosty in serving bowls. Serve chilled.

Nutritional Value (Amount per Serving):

- Calories 342
- Fat 34 g
- Carbohydrates 6.3 g
- Sugar 1 g
- Protein 2.9 g
- Cholesterol 123 mg

Strawberry Mousse

Preparation Time: 10 minutes
Cooking Time: 5 minutes
Serve: 4

Ingredients:

- 1 cup heavy whipping cream
- 1 cup fresh strawberries, chopped
- 2 tbsp Swerve
- 1 cup cream cheese

Directions:

1. Add heavy whipping cream in a large bowl and beat until thickened using hand mixer.
2. Add sweetener and cream cheese and beat well.
3. Add strawberries and fold well.
4. Pour in serving glasses and place in the refrigerator for 1-2 hours.
5. Serve chilled and enjoy.

Nutritional Value (Amount per Serving):

- Calories 320
- Fat 31.4 g
- Carbohydrates 6.2 g
- Sugar 1.9 g
- Protein 5.2 g
- Cholesterol 105 mg

Cheesecake Mousse

Preparation Time: 10 minutes
Cooking Time: 5 minutes
Serve: 6

Ingredients:

- 1 cup heavy whipping cream
- 1 tsp vanilla
- ¼ cup erythritol
- 8 oz cream cheese, softened

Directions:

1. Add the cream cheese in mixing bowl and beat until smooth.
2. Add vanilla and sweetener and stir to combine.
3. In another bowl, beat heavy whipping cream until stiff peaks form.
4. Fold whipped cream into the cream cheese mixture and beat using a hand mixer until fluffy. Place in refrigerator for 2 hours.
5. Pipe in serving glasses and serve chilled.

Nutritional Value (Amount per Serving):

- Calories 203
- Fat 20.6 g
- Carbohydrates 11.7 g
- Sugar 10.2 g
- Protein 3.3 g
- Cholesterol 69 mg

Delicious Berry Cheese Dessert

Preparation Time: 10 minutes
Cooking Time: 10 minutes
Serve: 8

Ingredients:

- 1 ½ lb ricotta cheese
- 1 cup blackberries
- 1 cup blueberries
- 1 cup raspberries
- 1 ½ tsp vanilla
- ½ cup erythritol
- 1 tbsp lemon zest
- ¼ cup heavy cream

Directions:

1. Add ricotta, vanilla, sweetener, and heavy cream in mixing bowl and using hand mixer beat until smooth.
2. In four serving cups layer alternating ricotta mixture and ¼ cup berries.
3. Serve and enjoy.

Nutritional Value (Amount per Serving):

- Calories 201
- Fat 12 g
- Carbohydrates 9 g
- Sugar 4 g
- Protein 10 g
- Cholesterol 32 mg

Chocó Peanut Butter Fudge

Preparation Time: 10 minutes
Cooking Time: 10 minutes
Serve: 16

Ingredients:

- ½ cup peanut butter
- ½ tsp vanilla
- ¼ cup Swerve
- 2 ½ tbsp unsweetened cocoa powder
- ¼ cup ghee

Directions:

1. Line small baking dish with parchment paper and set aside.
2. Add ghee in peanut butter in microwave-safe bowl and microwave until ghee and peanut butter is melted.
3. Add remaining ingredients and stir everything well and pour in prepared baking dish.
4. Place in refrigerator for 1 hour or until set.
5. Cut into pieces and serve.

Nutritional Value (Amount per Serving):

- Calories 78
- Fat 7.4 g
- Carbohydrates 2.1 g
- Sugar 0.8 g
- Protein 2.2 g
- Cholesterol 8 mg

Raspberry Fat Bombs

Preparation Time: 5 minutes
Cooking Time: 5 minutes
Serve: 8

Ingredients:

- ½ cup fresh raspberries
- 3 tbsp Swerve
- 2 tbsp coconut oil, melted
- 8 oz cream cheese, softened

Directions:

1. Add all ingredients into the food processor and process until smooth.
2. Pour fat bomb mixture into the mini muffin mold and place it in the refrigerator for 45 minutes.
3. Serve and enjoy.

Nutritional Value (Amount per Serving):

- Calories 134
- Fat 13.3 g
- Carbohydrates 2.4 g
- Sugar 0.4 g
- Protein 2.2 g
- Cholesterol 31 mg

Quick Lemon Mug Cake

Preparation Time: 5 minutes
Cooking Time: 2 minutes
Serve: 1

Ingredients:

- 1 egg, lightly beaten
- ½ tsp lemon rind
- 1 tbsp butter, melted
- 1 ½ tbsp fresh lemon juice
- 2 tbsp erythritol
- ¼ tsp baking powder, gluten-free
- ¼ cup almond flour

Directions:

1. In a small bowl, mix together almond flour, baking powder, and sweetener.
2. Add egg, lemon juice, and melted butter in almond flour mixture and whisk until well combined.
3. Pour cake mixture into the microwave-safe mug and microwave for 90 seconds.
4. Serve and enjoy.

Nutritional Value (Amount per Serving):

- Calories 385
- Fat 32 g
- Carbohydrates 8 g
- Sugar 1 g
- Protein 13 g
- Cholesterol 195 mg

Smooth & Silky Tiramisu Mousse

Preparation Time: 5 minutes

Cooking Time: 5 minutes

Serve: 2

Ingredients:

- ½ cup mascarpone cheese
- 1 tbsp erythritol
- 1 tsp unsweetened cocoa powder

Directions:

1. Add all ingredients into the blender and blend until smooth.
2. Pour blended mixture into the piping bag and pipe in serving glasses.
3. Place in refrigerator for 1 hour.
4. Serve chilled and enjoy.

Nutritional Value (Amount per Serving):

- Calories 110
- Fat 8.2 g
- Carbohydrates 2.4 g
- Sugar 0.2 g
- Protein 7.2 g
- Cholesterol 32 mg

Conclusion

This book guides you on how to adapt the keto diet after the age of 50 and what are the health benefits of the diet. My goal here is that provides you all related information about keto diet after age 50.

In this book, you will get 79 delicious and healthy keto recipes that are easy to prepare.

www.ingramcontent.com/pod-product-compliance
Lightning Source LLC
Chambersburg PA
CBHW081402070526
44583CB00020B/2649